Kate,
May Love
Sustain Ye
Blessings

Intuition

A Practical Yet Spiritual Guide

Originated by:
     Janine Baryza-Ly
Edited by:
     Dararith Ly
Cover by:
     Jill M. LeFevre

Janine Baryza-Ly
Website: www.AQuestForTruth.com

Table of Contents

Forward:

I am a Psychic Medium. Or at least that's what I have been calling myself. I have never really liked the words psychic, clairvoyant or any of these fortune telling words associated with what I do for work. I do gravitate towards the word Mystic, or even the phrase **I am that I am**. However that does not describe what it is that I do if you were to come see me. The truth is I am extremely intuitive. So, on all my business cards I call myself a Psychic Medium. Two simple words that for this day in age, seem to describe a person who can see the past, present, future and the beyond (loved ones who have passed, angels, guides and any other divine beings out there).

We are all psychic, we all have this intuitive ability. We use it all the time with out knowing it. Even more often, we stuff our intuitive voice into our stomachs and talk ourselves out of this inner communication that is trying to help guide us through out this spiritual journey called life. You know the voice that I speak of. It is the voice that tells you to leave a very well paying job (that we don't like), or break up with a boyfriend who seems perfectly good. It is that voice that tells us not to trust someone, or to talk to the stranger in the supermarket. This voice is yearning to be heard. When we do **not** listen to it, drama tends to be created so that we can get to a point when we have to surrender and listen. This intuitive voice reminds us that if we trust it we have the opportunity to open up to a whole new way to live. A life with purpose, meaning and above all, a life that lets us know that we truly are loved and guided.

What is this inner voice, what is your intuition? Who is actually talking to you? Where does all this come from? One answer - GOD. Yahweh, I am that I am. It is not a finite definition, but the information comes from a place of love. That is why your personal intuition speaks to what is for your best and highest good. Inside you know that you should listen to this guidance, to the God speaking to you, however you may not be sure how to start.

There are many theories about how a person becomes psychic. Some think there is a "secret" that you can learn to open up to this realm. There are those who believe that only a select few have the "gift" of psychic intuition. I am going to tell you how each and every one can become a highly intuitive individual. The secret to being Psychic, to being extremely intuitive, is to **Trust** and to practice trusting. That is it. It is cultivating the skill of your **Trust in God**.

We all are on a spiritual journey and in my opinion, the only reason to develop and cultivate your intuition is to travel on that path. It is to have union with Yahweh. It is the knowing of God through your being vs. your mind. No one really "needs" a psychic reading. If you cultivate your own personal intuitive connection and trust in your own inner voice your spiritual journey will unfold before you in a way that the "need" for a psychic, clairvoyant, or anything else truly won't be there. However we are human.

We are human and the help from other people is needed on our path. A psychic reading can be extremely healing, broadening your possibilities of life and allowing you to experience what your soul has been calling for. If done "right" a reading is a communication **not** built from pain, drama, mind and opinion, but a communication built on love, respect and TRUTH. It is a communication that does not speak to your mind, but rather your soul. It is the God in you talking to the God in another. The type of communication that we know exists, yet due to our humanness is often hard to harness. We often see through our distorted lens that has held onto our abandonment, hurt and perception. An intuitive conversation, taps into the love part of ourselves, the God part and we speak in the way that is for our best and highest good and the best and highest good of those around us. We are going to learn to trust a place of love for which our dialogue will be healing, purposeful and help develop our soul advancement. That should and will be your only motivation to learn these skills. To speak from Love and act in Love.

What is God? God is Love. You will talk from

God.

Chapter 1:

YOU ARE PSYCHIC

Regarding our intuition, there is one thing that we all want to hear from someone other than ourselves; that someone else sees this extraordinary psychic gift in us. It's as if we are waiting for others to determine when or even if we will take the first steps in developing our own spirituality and intuition. This isn't the first time you will hear this and it won't be the last, but let me start off by telling you -

YOU are extremely intuitive, you should develop this gift that I see in you. It is amazing the talent that you hold inside yourself. Let's unlock that hidden divineness and let your light shine so bright so that all can see.

OK, with that out of the way, you have been discovered as one of the very special people who posses this spiritual alignment, allowing you to access parts of the universe that we cannot see with our eyes, but can read with our souls. You have been invited to see TRUTH. There are many different facets to developing the skills of a psychic and this book is going to give you practical advice and exercises that you can use to expand your intuition on this spiritual journey. These skills can be used for many different reasons, however I encourage that you use these skills, not to show the world that you can pull a rabbit out of a hat, but so that you can heal yourself, and in turn the world.

I also suggest that in conjunction with developing the psychic mind, that you are also developing the spiritual mind. Have some sort of daily spiritual or religious practice that grounds you and expands your soul. It is helpful to have a home base, a place in the spiritual realm that is safe, almost rote. A place that you don't need to think too hard to get to. For some this may be a ritual meditation, or a prayer. I was raised in the Catholic tradition, and although I have studied a plethora of different religions, modalities and practices, it is my Catholic base that keeps me grounded. It is a base, from which I can branch out and start to know God in an intuitive way.

Your First Step Today and Everyday is to Say an I AM statement.

I **AM** extremely intuitive **And So It IS**

I **AM** a psychic medium **And So It IS**

I **AM** clairvoyant **And So It IS**

I **AM** divinely inspired daily **And So It IS**

I **AM** a mystic **And So It IS**

I **AM** prophetic **And So It IS**

I AM THAT I AM

IAM_____

_____**And So It IS**

(Please fill in the blank.)

Now this statement is very powerful - it is a statement that you are making to yourself, to your soul. You are calling forth your true, powerful, and creative nature. You are speaking in the words of GOD. You are proclaiming who you are and you are substantiating it by saying that it is so. You are speaking in a divine manor. So I encourage you to use this I AM statement in other aspects of your life.

You have called to your spirit who you are and what you are capable of. How powerful! Stand in that power, for a moment. Stop and feel the sensation. Let it seep through your entire body and imagine that your whole being is shining. Halos aren't just for angels you know.

CHAPTER 2:

A PRAYER OF PROTECTION and ALIGNING YOURSELF.

OK, you are starting to open yourself up to a world that is unknown to you. I would love to say that it is always benevolent soft and beautiful, however I would not be speaking the truth. There are things out there that are not for your best and highest good. If you are not careful, you can allow that into your life. When we go into this intuitive realm we start to deal with energy. Everything is energy and has an energetic element. The nice part of this, is if you experience something that does not speak to your best and highest good, you have the ability and power to change it. I am going to give you a few options to protect yourself from unwanted energy, as well as align yourself to the Highest of the High, to GOD, and to trust that you are always acting in and with LOVE.

Prayer of Protection

This is my favorite prayer. Not only does it just feel good, but I can actually see it working as well. I share this prayer with anyone and everyone who is willing to hear it. Here is how the prayer goes;

The light of God surrounds me

The love of God enfolds me

The power of God protects me

The presence of God watches over me

Where ever I am God is.

This is how the prayer works; you say the prayer three times. As you say the prayer you envision a ball of Gods love and light surrounding you. It covers every aspect of you; you are now in and with God. You are **protected** by the highest of the high and the infinite. You are engulfed in the light, love and the protection of God. I love the word Yahweh so I also say this prayer with Yahweh instead of God, it speaks more to me personally.

Another way to protect yourself, is to imagine that you are in a golden circle that completely encompasses you.   As you are in this golden circle pray or say; *Only what is for your best and highest good can come in this golden circle and what is for others' best and highest good can leave this golden circle.*   This is a simple yet effective way to protect yourself as well as those around you.

You can surround yourself with white light.   Or pick a color of your choice, that speaks to you and envision an eggshell like surface surrounding you. Again only what is for your best and highest good is allowed to come in and only what is for the best and highest good of those around you can come out of your shell or white light. These are just a few different ways to protect yourself, however there are many, many others, please feel free to choose which ever one that speaks to you the most and that is simple for you to perform or imagine.

Aligning Yourself

What do I mean aligning yourself? When we think of the beyond, the spirit world and all the unexplained energy fields that we may be able to tap into, you must realize that just as on earth, not all of it is for your best and highest good. Just like here in the physical realm you have your Gandhi's and you have your Charlie Manson's. I would love to get the wisdom from a Gandhi energy, however I would be very afraid to access Charlie Manson. This is why we need to align ourselves not only for our best and highest good, but also engulf ourselves in the light and love of God, Yahweh.

Personally, I don't like to talk about the negative side to intuition. However I do feel that it is a great injustice to not acknowledge that all information isn't good information. And this is where the spiritual component to yourself comes into play. If you are looking to **wow** people with your skills, you run a higher risk to aligning yourself with something that may not be of the highest nature. As people manipulate each other for vanity and fame, so too can it happen in this realm of things. This is why I feel that it is so important that you develop a strong spiritual faith and a regular practice, if you are to truly do this type of work for others.

So how do you align yourself to God, the highest of the high, the infinite, almighty energy? Sit in a chair with your feet flat on the floor, put your palms up and close your eyes. Imagine that there is this strong powerful light beaming from the top of your head. Shoot that light up all the way beyond, what you think is possible and connect to the God. Only have one huge and strong light line from you to God and just bask in the nature of this energy. Then ask/pray; *Dear God I ask that all the information that I receive is for my best and highest good and for the best and highest good of those around me. I ask that all my information be from the truest and purest source and that only light and love come from my mouth, my body and my aura. Thank you for helping me today and thank you for allowing the information to come through me, not from me. This thy will, not my will. Thank you God and So It Is.*

Realize that angels, guides, ascended masters, spirits, loved ones who have crossed, etc... they all fall UNDER God. So go to the source first, then if any of those come through, then you know where and how they came to you, and you now can be sure that you are wrapped in the protection and sanctuary of God. You can not read angels if you don't use the word God. I have read books, seen cards and heard of many people who talk to angels. That is great, however many do not reference or acknowledge that Angels are the messengers of

God. So go to God first, and then let the angels come.

If you take the first part of this book seriously enough, then you really don't need any more information. Aligning yourself, trusting, and a practical spiritual framework, are the key ingredients to walking on your spiritual path with true purpose and wonderment. This intuitive, personal relationship with God is where all things are possible and a boundless world begins. Standing in this power allows you to trust in your own information and be content with not knowing everything, but knowing you are where you are suppose to be at this very moment.

Chapter 3:

WHAT AN INTUITIVE READING MAY ENTAIL

Ever wonder what is really being read when you go see a psychic? As you embark on your intuitive journey what are you reading off of someone else? Think of reading a story and each of us carry around our story in our bodies and our energy field. We all have a past, a present, a future - loved ones who have crossed over and spiritual help from the other side. All of this is around you, it is encoded above, below and in you. Your energetic persona holds all of this information. Picture it like an energy wave. For example, when you listen to music, you can not see the energy waves there, but somehow you do end up hearing a sound. It is the same way with a reading. You may not be able to see the vibration that you are picking up, however that vibration exists and you are able to tune into it.

The beautiful part of a reading is that you (if aligned correctly) can pick up on this vibration, not through the subjective perspective of the person you are reading, but from an objective perspective, giving them an outside, non-judgmental truth of what is around them. Have you ever had a friend that has low self esteem, however when you see or think of them you can see all the greatness they hold with in themselves? When we give a reading to someone we are seeing what they may not be able to see. Often times, their vision is blurred by past experiences, emotional imbalance or genetic code. You are unlocking and bringing to light someone's true nature and allowing them to see it for themselves. That is very powerful! You are able to see a situation in your mind's eye and see what energy is there, not reading what the person is thinking, but beyond the mind and into Truth.

Another type of reading is a mediumship reading. With this type of reading, you may experience loved ones who have passed, angels or guides. When I first started out receiving this type of information, I would question if that person (who has passed) was really around, or if I was just reading someone's memories.

I then had very profound experience where I was doing a reading for a friend's grandmother. During this reading I had her grandmother, my friend and her sister. The Grandfather (who had passed on) immediately came through and I gave all sorts of information to each one of them. I was able to see this grandfather through the eyes of the grandmother, my friend and her younger sister. But then I saw the grandfather, in his truest nature, standing on the right side of me. I could see that it was really him, that it was something beyond memories or even perception from the three of them. I saw his energy, who his soul truly is. I was so honored and delighted to have had that experience, for it gave me an even deeper meaning as to who we are and that we never die. Whenever you question yourself, please ask for the truth to come and then accept that knowledge.

Chapter Four:

Giving a Reading

Ever since you could talk, you were taught to think before speaking. Giving a reading goes completely against what we have been taught. Your focus, your objective, is to give true information to another. In order to give TRUE information, you must have as little judgment and "thinking" as possible. What happens when you "think" during a reading is that often times we can talk ourselves out of what we are receiving because through our experiences the information does not make any sense. When receiving information for another, the information is not for your benefit. This means that more often than not, the information will not make "sense" to you, but will resonate with the person who is receiving the reading. One of the best ways to bypass thinking too much is to speak the very moment an image, smell, touch, etc. comes to you. You are always acting with integrity if you are relaying exactly how you are receiving the information. If you have aligned yourself to read what is for a person's best and highest good, you are receiving information that the person needs; not what they want. This may be the hardest part of being intuitive - Giving information that may not be wanted at the time, but may prove helpful to them on their path.

Many shy away from this type of work just because of this aspect of the job. Or overwhelmed with compassionate hearts, some do not give the TRUE information to the client. You must trust in yourself and the bond you have built with your faith to relay information to another in the truest form that you know how. Having said all that, explain to the client, that they do not have to agree or listen to what you have said. The client needs to use their own discretion on what information speaks truth to them and what does not. You should always stay in your own integrity and truth, so that your skill can consistently be developed.

There are many reasons why you receive the information that you do. There was a period of time in my life that whenever I went to get a reading, the information was always off, or just plain wrong. I had gotten frustrated that all my readings seemed to be so far off and I knew that I should do the opposite of whatever advice I was given. It wasn't until one day in my spiritual development that I realized why my readings were going in that manner. At the time, I was in a rebellious phase. I would do the opposite of whatever someone had told me. So in truth I was getting a perfect reading, because I was receiving information in a manner to get me to remain on my path. I received the information in a way that got me to react and do what was for my best and highest good. I use this story as an example of why you cannot judge yourself when embarking in this field, yet immerse yourself in creating spiritual roots that will ground you as you explore these new facets of life.

Judgment

We all make judgments. We have judged others and have been judged ourselves. Due to this fact, most of us try to hide our true nature. It is OK for a person to judge you under false pretenses; however it is far too risky for us to allow ourselves to be vulnerable to have someone judge who we truly are. This is why most of us create walls or present ourselves in a manner that is not always true. In order for a client to feel truly comfortable with you and for you to feel comfortable with yourself, you must leave your judgment at the door. The less you judge the less you will be judged.

Also, if you have a particular opinion or are too judgmental, your information will probably reflect not what TRUTH is, but what you want to see.

Judgment is energy that confuses the mind because it is not based in TRUTH but rather in some sort of insecurity, fear or falsehood. When you judge, you try to convince yourself or another that you know best, or that you know more about them and their ways than they do. When you are judged it stops your own intuitive energy and makes you spend a lot of time discerning the TRUTH. It takes work and trust in "thy" self for the mind to let go of what it is being told vs. what it knows in its heart. To trust thyself is to trust GOD, for you are made in the image of him. To trust in man more than GOD, you are serving a false God. To trust the judgment that money, status and the size of your house depicts if you are "good" or not is abomination of any intuition or love that is within yourself. You only judge for fear that someone else may have a better life than you. However, if you were truly happy and at peace, you wouldn't care what anyone else was doing. You may ask, what about God's judgment? Does God Judge? Obviously, I can't give you that answer. Since we don't know what God's plan truly is, how do we know if he would judge? It makes more sense to me that He is an advocate for our freedom and our spirit to know him, and in that place there can be no judgment. YOUR LIFE is not about things, travel, degrees and money. YOUR LIFE is about the ability to know yourself and accept others so that you can live in spiritual freedom together, trust in each others energy as well as cultivate your own relationship to the beyond. Nothing else matters, nothing else is based in this truth. Love today and accept those around you, because they are exactly where they are supposed to be.

Practice accepting others for all their faults and imperfections, accept those aspects in yourself, and the clearer your information will become. Intuition is truly a spiritual path, and an opportunity to become who and what you truly are; a loving and companionate being. All these aspects to reading are skills. Skills do not happen overnight, so do not expect to wake up perfect tomorrow, yet practice and work at it and you will be amazed at what parts of yourself you will

reveal.

CHAPTER 5:

RECEIVING THE INFORMATION

How do you receive the information?

We are all different. Just as you may be better in math than in social studies, how you receive your information may come through better in one way than another. That is why there are so many different techniques and skills that you can develop to optimally access that intuitive side to your self. We also all have different interests and focuses in our own life, so we will have different focuses that we can access when being in the intuitive realm. For instance, when you read someone you may notice that all you really want to talk about is their childhood. Or you keep seeing images of what they were in a past life. Maybe all you want to talk about is their love life, or you see people around them that have passed. These are all just niches. You can still access other parts of the person, but you just may be better at one thing over another.

Using your Five Senses

This is the "how" in receiving information. Use all five of your senses to collect the energy and information. We all have different learning styles, and we all have different ways of receiving our intuition. As you allow the information to come through to you, be mindful of which senses are being receptive so you can begin to build an awareness of where you are personally in order to enhance your own progress.

Sight

You may hear a psychic say "I see..." and you maybe asking yourself, do they really see that in the physical form, or the mental form. I believe that there are people who can see ghosts in more of the physical form, however that is another whole subject so I am going to explain what "seeing" is with in a psychic reading.

I want you to think of the house you grew up in as a child. I specifically want you to remember what your room looked like when you were 15. In your mind's eye, I want you to see your room, see your bed, the posters on the wall, how the furniture is laid out, what color was your bed spread? What was on your bed, where are your cloths kept? Are they in the closet? How about the dresser? Where did you keep your diary? Can you look into that diary and read a page?

As you are going through this exercise you are "seeing". It is almost like a memory, yet instead of you thinking of a specific event you are accessing what things looked like and you can see that as you ask yourself more detailed questions more details come into, that seeing part of your brain. When a psychic talks about what they "see", it normally is in this type of fashion, almost like a memory, yet a bit more in the here and now.

Touch

The touch part of an intuitive reading. I must say that it is much more rare that I find psychics talk about this sense in their readings. I believe that it is because it seems to be a bit scary for people to be physically touched by something that they may not be able to totally identify. For me the only times that I have been physically touched has been through a mediumship reading. When I say a mediumship reading I am talking about when I have loved ones who have crossed over, or guides, angels, teachers, etc. When I feel touched it more often than not just feels like an intense mass of energy near me. Sometimes I can feel someone touch my hand, or a full body mass of energy standing next to me or behind me. I have also just felt heat all over my body.

Although I mainly feel heat, others feel it as cold. Either way it is an overwhelming sense of physically feeling something in the room with you. If you do start to physically "feel" something around you, I want you to close your eyes and imagine what that energy looks like, I want you describe whether it is big, or small, thick or thin, old or young. What does that energy feel like to you.

Taste

Taste is fun, if you are like me and love food. So how do you taste something, that you truly aren't eating?

I want you to think of your favorite meal, something you really like. Now close your eyes and imagine yourself eating that meal, get so wrapped up in eating it that you can actually start tasting the food in your mouth. Feel the texture of the food, the temperature, is it hot, is it cold, sweet or savory. How does it feel as it is going down your throat? How do you feel as your eating it? This mind tasting is the way an intuitive taste feels like.

Hear

Second to sight, I believe that many "hear" intuitive messages. They can come when you are fully awake, when you are asleep, or in that in-between stage. There are various forms of "hearing".

One form is that voice inside your head. You know the one, the voice that tells you that you don't like a person or to get out of a bad relationship. Then there is another type of hearing, where you actually hear a voice, a distinct voice. This sometimes can make you feel as if you are crazy, but as long as you know you are of sound mind, this is true communication between you and another realm, whether it be a loved one who has passed, or an angel, a guide, God etc.

Smell

Close your eyes, think of your favorite flower, what does that smell like? Smell it with your mind's eye. Now I want you to think of your mom's home cooking. What is your favorite meal that you remember she made? When you step inside the house remember that smell that gets you excited. Can you describe that smell? This is how you psychically smell.

Feeling Empathically

I know that this is not one of the five senses, yet I feel as if it is the strongest, yet most overlooked way to recognize your intuition. As soon as you sit next to or talk to a person, I want you to immediately recognize how you feel. When you see them or think of them, how do you feel? Are they sad,? Happy? Angry? Depressed? When you look at them or are around them does your shoulder hurt, or do you have any pain anywhere in your body?   Pay attention to how you personally feel, and then ask yourself, is how I feel from you or is it from someone else who you are around?

I will give you an example. Let's say you woke up today, you're feeling pretty good, and you do your normal morning rituals and go about your day. All of a sudden your phone rings and it's your friend, you pick up the phone and your friend starts telling you about how they were just dumped by their significant other and that they where really upset and thought that person was the one they were going to marry. You as a good friend console them and tell them there are plenty of fish in the sea and that you never really liked that person anyway. Your friend thanks you for helping them feel better, and you decide that you guys will meet up later, but right now you got to get ready for work, so you hang up the phone. You go about your day and get to work and just about in the middle of the day, you start to feel really sad. Your not sure why, but you're upset and angry and are starting to have a bad day. This is called being empathetic, you can actually feel and take on what someone else is going through. Many of us do this without any conscious effort or knowledge that we are doing it. It is a great eye opening experience once you can start to identify if your "feelings" are truly yours or belong to someone else around you.

If you start to pay attention to this, you can be a very strong healer and helper to those around you. Because you will be able to relate and help others with the knowledge that it is not you or from you, you won't need to take on so much energetically, but still be able to put it in a place where it can be healed. I believe that having this empathic ability is so compassionate and psychic, yet sometimes the hardest to identify. With practice the way you view life can be so enlightening.

These are all different ways to receive information, utilize all your senses and

see where you receive the most information. Acknowledging how you receive will help you cultivate your skill to develop your intuition.

Chapter 6:

Exercises

In this chapter I am going to give you a set of exercises and ideas for you to practice your intuition, both by yourself and with others. Know that you always have an opportunity to tap into this part of yourself at all times, it is up to you how much you want to.

Practicing your intuition when you are alone:

1) Listen to psychic shows where psychics provide live readings. There are many radio shows where a psychic is giving live readings on air. Listen to their shows and as a person calls up to get a reading, write down the information that you have received when listening to the person and see if what you picked up is correct. Obviously not all of your information will be confirmed, but you will be amazed at how much you may have picked up. One link that I know that has many live psychic readers is: blogtalkradio.com.

2) As a passenger on a long car ride, try to hone into what license plate numbers and letters are going to be on the next car that passes you. This is a fun game that you can play with kids as well.

It gets the intuition juices flowing as well as passes the time on a long drive. You can use this exercise in a variety of ways. You can see if you can sense where the next police car may be, or what color car will pass you, or what type of cargo a truck maybe carrying. Use your imagination. However I suggest that you only use one of these variations at a time, so that you are better focused.

3) When you wake up in the morning, write down all the people who pop into your head that will call you that day. See how many of those people actually do. As you get more advanced, see if you can pin point a time that they will call.

4) Tap into the world around you   Sit by yourself and see if you can intuitively receive what is going on in the world. Read newspapers and watch the TV for confirmation.   Can you predict what the headline news for your area will be? Can you see the focus of what the global news will look like for this week? I have a very intuitive friend who kept on getting the feeling that she should not shop at this one supermarket. For weeks she kept on seeing a man kidnapping a woman. She stayed clear of the store. A few weeks later she read the news paper and saw that a woman had gone missing from that very same location. Through many experiences she realized that much of her information that she was receiving had to do with events that was in her local newspaper. This information allowed her to explore using her intuitive gifts to help fight crime.

5) Record your dreams. If you are a dreamer, write down your dreams and then be aware of what is around you. Many times, dreams need to be interpreted. You are often the focus of the dream, so make sure that you record the "feeling" the dream aroused as well as any seemingly important details. If you dream about someone else you know, share your dream with them. Although it may not make any sense to you, the dream may have significance to them. Or sometimes you may just be picking up that that person needs someone to reach out to them. Dreams are a lot of fun, pay attention.

I receive a lot of my information through my dreams and I have learned to listen to them. The more I started to listen to my dreams the more information came through that channel. I do not only receive information for myself, but for others as well. For example I had a dream where everyone who I had gone to high school with was re uniting. It felt different than a reunion, but everyone was catching up on how their lives had been. I knew that there was a particular reason we were all getting together, but I wasn't sure what for. There was a great warm energy around the dream and I even knew as I was dreaming that I not received the whole story. The next morning I had woken up and got a call that an old classmate of mine had passed away and that everyone was getting together to go to the wake.

Another time I dreamt of a great celebration for an old friend of mine. I just knew that he must be getting married. When I called him up to tell him about my dream, sure enough he was engaged and planning the wedding.

There is such a wondrous adventure in dreaming. It has personally been my most amazing portal of information. I have no judgment and no expectation; I find lucid dreaming to be a great freedom from this paradigm into another. As with everything the more you accept, the more you will gain.

To practice with someone else:

1) Spend time with your elders. The longer you have lived the more experiences, loved ones who have passed, and more expansive stories you have to tell. Spend time with one of your elders, see what information you have received when sitting with them, and then ask them to tell you their story. It is so nice to be around someone who has lived, they have such great wisdom. They normally don't need you to tell them what they have gone through, but would love to tell you their story.

2) Everyone has a past, a present and a future. When practicing we want to start with things that can be confirmed. The best way to start off is to tell someone a story of their childhood. You can start off by making things up, you will be surprised how your imagined story, at some point starts to make sense.

I realize often times as I read someone's past that I will tend to pick up on certain points of time, where there was a big impact on the way that person views their life. I regularly pick up information when a person needs to be healed. I had a regular massage therapy client, who would come in once a week for me to work on her chronic hip pain. She had this pain for many years: went to the chiropractor three times a week, tried various different mattresses, shoes, and techniques. She tried as hard as she could to relieve herself from this pain. One day as I was working on her, I decided to do some energy work on the hip area. I started to feel intense emotions and started to "see" her at a much younger age. When I was done with the work I knew that this hip problem was related to her past. (You must realize that she did not know that I was psychic and I was at my infant stage of development of my intuition). After we were done I asked her if she can remember anything that may have happened to that hip when she was a teenager. Then she started to tell me a story of how one day in high school someone had pushed her and she fell into a garbage can and hurt her hip. Everyone was laughing, even her best friend. The emotion was caught in her muscles. Although as an adult she can see how silly the moment was, it still had not been released or healed. At that time, she stuffed it inside and decided to forget all about it, rather than let it go. Up until that moment she had forgotten all about it, however her energetic and muscular self had not. Through this process she was able to see the root of the problem.

3) Then read what is going on with them in the present. Don't forget to pick up on their feelings, i.e. stressed, happy, sad, etc. See if you can sense what is going on from an outside perspective and give them another way to look at their current situation. As you are sitting with the person, allow yourself to say what your first impression of their attitude toward life is.

4) Read a person with the intention to have contact with their loved ones that have passed on. When you look at a person with this intention, who comes to mind first? Grandma? Mom? Sister? Brother? Dad? Uncle? Then try to explain that person's personality or maybe see if you can pick up on how they died. Does it feel like they passed from a sickness or an accident/ trauma? Are they showing you an object or talking about others they have left behind? Most loved ones come in just to say that they love the person and that they are helping them from the other side. Allow your mind to expand and feel the energy of that loved one around you or the person. The more the person who you are reading can confirm your information the more that you will be able to say. Many times it is great to have some sort of physical exchange, whether it be a handshake or a hug. There are many things that are beyond our words. If you have and feel a presence of love, allow yourself to transfer that purity to another that take both of you beyond interpretation and communicate in the most direct manor; soul to soul.

5) Reading past lives. Not everyone believes in past lives; but if they do, most associate themselves with another time period other than the present one. We can still be carrying residual trauma from another life time, which would be a reason that it is still in our energy field. Or it may be a time period one can learn from. Since a past life can not be confirmed with certainty, you must let the client know this is what you are picking up. See if you can read a person's past life, tell a story about that past life to them. More often than not, the "pattern" of the past life, will have significance to their life today.

6) Channeling Angels, Guides, Animal Guides, Ascended Masters, Etc. When contacting in this realm, remember to always ask what is for the best and highest good for the person you are reading. Ask these helpers questions and see what type of answers you get. Try not to interpret the answers but rather, say them as you are receiving them. Be the clearest channel that you can be. This means do not try to interpret, but just relay. Picture yourself as the messenger, you do not come up with the message yourself, but you just read what you have been given. Have a person ask you a question. Say the first thing that comes to your mind. Again speak before you think.

Channeling is a different energy - it is allowing something other than you to speak through you. As you channel, allow your body to relax, to align in a place where you feel safe and be free to let the energy flow through you. A way to channel is not only through the spoken word, but also through the written word. A great exercise in channeling is to sit in a quiet place with either a pen and paper or in front of the computer and ask for information, then just start typing. Do not judge what you are typing or try to put correct grammar or spelling to your words, just freely allow your fingers to have a mind of their own. Do not pay attention to what is being written, when you are done you can then read it. Often times you won't even remember what you have written. This exercise, if done alone, will often times give you messages that are for you and for your own spiritual growth.

There are many other ways to practice your intuition. Realize that you can and are doing this all the time. The more time you spend listening to your sixth sense, the more comfortable you will be with your gift and with trusting your own information. You are profoundly intuitive, it is up to you to make it a daily practice of listening, trusting and implementing your new self.

Chapter 7:

Clearing and Cleansing the Energy

Clearing and cleansing energy. Everything is and has energy. You are an energetic being, so are those around you. When you start to work on this level of intuition you are starting to work with energy. It is as if you are reading and putting words to energy. Because of this, it is important to clear all energy that is not your own out of your energy field. It is also important to clear the energy in the place you have been doing your work. You can also use the techniques that I am going to tell you about in your daily routine, at work, in your home and before and after you meditate. These are great ways to be more aware of your surroundings as well as keep your own channel clear.

Why clear the energy? Have you ever been around someone who is having a bad day? Then all of a sudden you start to feel sad or depressed? You are picking up on their energy and started to make it your own. When you delve into the realm where you are giving intuitive readings you are dealing with many levels of other peoples energy, emotions, losses, joys etc. You will be dealing with energy that is simply not yours. So in order for the true healing process to happen, you must own your energy and they must own theirs. This is why we clear and cleanse ourselves as well as recall our own energy that we may have given out and return energy that we may have picked up.

Clearing energy with tools and incense

There are many different incense's and tools you can use to clear energy. You can light a candle during your session. Fire has many interpretations; the simplest one is that it represents "the light",, cleaning the area of everything not pure. You can also energetically clear a room with bells, ringing bells through out the room changes the vibration of the energy in that space.

I prefer to clear energy with either sage, sandalwood, or nag champa. For cleansing energy, I prefer frankincense. I start at one point in a room and walk clockwise around the room, opening a window so that whatever energy does not belong has a place to go. You may find that people say that there is a certain scent that clears better than another, however I find that what will work best for you is to pick the scent that you most connect with. Again, heed your own intuition as to what will be for your best and highest good. This is a good practice to get into before and after you do any spiritual work on yourself or others.

Clearing others energy from your energy field.

A simple way to clear another's energy from yourself is to sit with your feet firmly on the ground, preferably with your shoes off. Repeat three times in a powerful yet calm voice,

"Anything not of thee, change me now and set

me free"

Salt is a great way to also cleanse the energy around you. Taking a bath with fifteen teaspoons of salt will help you change your vibration into a more balanced state. This is a great practice when you need help getting over your own personal hurtles and blocks as well as just over all balancing.

Calling Back Your own Energy

Throughout the day we give our energy out to people. When you are at work, at home, with your kids, your spouse, your friends, you are giving them a little piece of you. This is a normal process and you take a bit of energy from those same people. However, in order to truly heal ourselves we need to get to know who we are. In order to do this we need to create and harness all of our own energy. This technique makes you feel so full and exhilarated to be surrounded by who and what you know best, **YOU!** Although I have come to find this exercise takes a bit of practice to fully feel the benefits, you should feel different the first time you go through it. Also be aware of what emotions that may surface when you are calling yourself back to you.

Get in a comfortable position, sitting or laying down. Take a few deep breaths and get in to a nice meditative state. Imagine that you are this extremely powerful magnet, but the only thing that you attract is **your own** energy. You are such a powerful magnet that if your energy is anywhere in the world or in outer space, it still can not resist your magnetic pull. Then I want you to think of all the things you did that day, all the people you talked to, everything that you came in contact with and attract your energy back from those people, places and things. As you go through this exercise you may realize how much of your energy goes towards one certain project or person. As you call back your energy from these things see how it feels to regain your own power. Some people find it hard to reclaim their own energy, feelings and intentions. Others start to feel energized and revived, empowering themselves to truly be who and what they are. As you are attracting this energy back, put a filter on the top of your head that the energy must go through before it engulfs you. This filter, changes your own energy to be aligned to your best and highest good. It gets revitalized and shines brighter than you have ever imagined. As you refuel, you start glowing from top to bottom and feeling exhilaration and empowerment with being You. Take a moment to feel how great You are.

Use these techniques as often as you would like.

Again as with everything, the more you practice,

the more real and powerful they become. Enjoy

getting to know who you are.

Chapter 8:

How to Receive

If you want to know the secret to being a great giver is to become a great receiver. I find that most people really like to give, give, give, yet they become very uncomfortable when it is their time to receive. It is the healer who gives healings all day, but won't go to get a healing. It is the caretaker who takes care of everyone, but won't allow anyone to cook them a meal. It is the massage therapist who works all day, yet never receives a massage. All these examples are people who are out of balance and who are not working to their full potential. Just remember you will only be able to give as much as you are able to receive when it comes to the energetic realm. The more comfortable you are with who you are, the more you will allow others around you to become more comfortable with themselves.

If your intention is to be a great psychic, well then you better go and experience many psychic readings. The better you become with opening yourself to be "read" the more others will be comfortable to open themselves up to you. I have found that my best readings aren't due to my ability to give, but rather the other person's ability to receive. Heal yourself and you will be able to heal others.

When I speak of receiving I am not talking about taking energy (sucking) from others. In order to receive, especially in an intuitive way, means that you have started to accept your imperfections and realize how perfect these imperfections are. What I mean is that you have become less fearful of your faults and of your greatness. You are ready to have truth be spoken to you and do not try to block what you do not want to hear. The ability to receive is the ability to love yourself and acknowledge your own power to change.

This is harder than you may think. I am asking you to find the pain behind the anger, and then find the love behind the pain. It is about stopping the self loathing and the guilt that we hold inside and perhaps more importantly, allowing others to help in that process. It is about showing your weaknesses as well as your strengths. This is the time to not be afraid of who you are, but see that you are loved and cared for. Allow yourself to love yourself. It is about accepting the responsibility of the sacred life that you have been given.

And then finally, allow yourself to see the God in you. Be able to accept how truly powerful you are and use this power with humility and grace so that you can become a healer in the truest sense of the word. A healer is one that heals by being, not doing. Stay in truth and honesty and others will feel the freedom to do the same. You are loved.

Chapter 9:

Have Fun On Your Spiritual Path!

I am so excited that you are interested in this journey. Remember that just as you are unique in the way you look, where you came from and who you are, so too are you unique in the way you receive your intuitive information. Have fun with this path and trust that you are always where you are supposed to be. Explore beyond what you have imagined possible and realize that you are a special individual, so trust who and what you are. When things get to be too serious, realize that you are supposed to be having fun! Find the fun and be open to anything! Live, Love, and spread Joy! Peace to you all and thank you.

A Prayer of Thanks

Thank you God for this day,
For today is a new beginning, a new life
I feel your presence surrounding me and your love
engulfing my soul
I walk in your footsteps and I answer your call
I am thankful

Thank you God for this day,
For today I see the good in all people,
I see the God in others and allow the God in me to be
shown
I walk with grace and listen to your guidance
I am thankful

Thank you God for this day,
For today is a miracle
I am at peace
I walk with love and act with compassion
I Am That I Am
Amen